Saint Francis of Assisi

WRITTEN & ILLUSTRATED BY TIM LADWIG

PARACLETE PRESS
Brewster, Massachusetts

2021 First Printing

Saint Francis of Assisi

Copyright © 2022 by Tim Ladwig

ISBN 978-1-64060-552-7

The Paraclete Press name and logo (dove on cross) are trademarks of Paraclete Press.

Library of Congress Control Number: 2021944712

10 9 8 7 6 5 4 3 2 1

Published by Paraclete Press
Brewster, Massachusetts
www.paracletepress.com

Manufactured by PRINPIA Co., Ltd.
54, Gasanro 9-Gil, Geumcheon-gu, Seoul 08513, Korea.
Printed in September 2021, Seoul, South Korea.

Contents

ong ago in 1182, there were wars among walled towns of Italy, each seeking to gain power and wealth. Young soldiers rode out the city gates with hopes of winning the glory of knighthood. Some returned from battle as knights. Others never again entered those gates alive.

In the town of Assisi, its buildings made of pink stone quarried from the overlooking Mount Subasio, a baby boy was born.

The baby's mother, Pica Bernardone, had him baptized in the San Rufino Cathedral as Giovanni, Italian for John. His father, Pietro Bernardone, was a merchant of fine cloth, and at the time of Giovanni's baptism he was away on business in France. Perhaps he was very successful there, because on returning home he gave his baby son the name Francesco—which was a kind of nickname. In Italian this meant "little Frenchman." We might say "Frenchy."

As a boy, Francis ran with his friends through the steep, narrow passages of Assisi, pretending to be soldiers, or just seeking fun and adventure. When they reached a terrace near the top of the city wall, they could look out over steep hills with olive trees and vineyards in the valley far below.

Like other, larger towns with a bishop, Assisi was proud of its beautiful cathedral, the bishop's seat, made glorious inside with the work of famous painters and glittering mosaics.

Priests were responsible for smaller parish churches such as San Damiano. Inside that church was a simple crucifix image of Jesus painted on linen cloth glued to a walnut cross. Years later, God would use that image to speak to the young man Francis.

As Francis grew, his love of life and adventure made him a leader of the fun-loving, adventurous young men in town. Because of his father's love of France and his successful business dealing in fine cloth, Francis had coins in his money pouch and dressed in colorful French fashions. He was liked by all but he did not think himself better than others because of the bright clothes. As for being wealthy, Francis spent his money more easily on others than on himself. Whenever he saw a need, he cared for it. His mother didn't know what to think of Francis. She would say he was more like a prince than a son.

If a prince, Francis was one that thought every person was of royal blood. One day while selling fabric at his father's booth in the crowded Assisi market, he was caught between two people talking to him at once: a man wanting to buy, and a beggar asking for coins. Francis was torn between the two. He finished business with the buyer and then bolted after the beggar, finding him on a winding, narrow street. He handed the poor man more money than the surprised fellow could ever hope for. Francis, standing in the narrow street, made a vow to God never to turn away a poor man. And he never did.

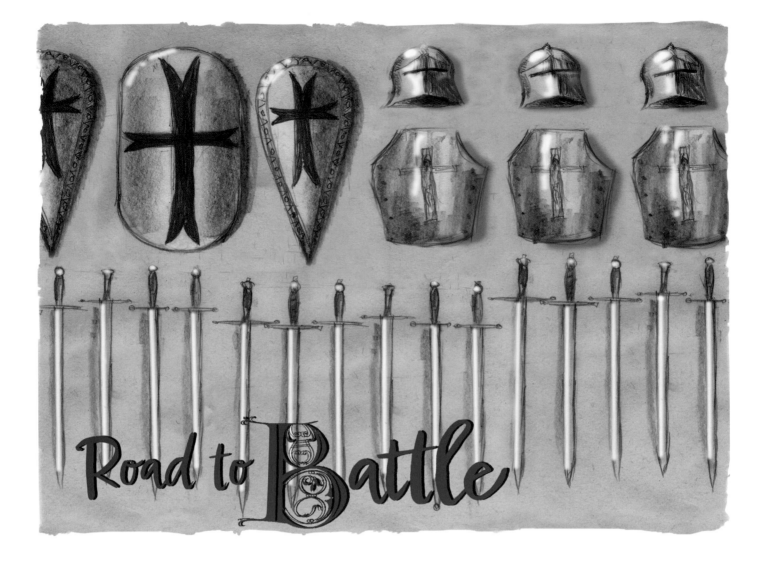

Road to Battle

At the age of twenty, young Francis joined Assisi's army to fight against nearby Perugia. He and some fellow soldiers were taken as captives and thrown into a dungeon. The cold, heat, hunger, and sickness did not dishearten Francis, who kept up the spirits of each of his fellow prisoners by his own cheerfulness—even treating the one suspected of being a traitor the same as the others. Francis withstood prison for almost a year, but then he became sick and could only lie down, shaking with a fever.

Finally, his father was able to pay a ransom to free him. Out of the dungeon and through Assisi's city gate he returned. When he was in his own home again, his mother did her best to see that her son recovered from his sickness and regained his strength.

When it seemed he was well enough to fight again, Francis eagerly bought a suit of armor and an especially fine warrior's mantle, a sort of cape worn over his armor for warmth. Later, he happened across a very poor man and exchanged his own beautiful mantle for the man's shabby cloak.

In his bed that night, Francis had a vision of swords, shields, and armor hung in an armory. The swords were made in the shape of a cross, like Crusaders' swords. The shields and armor also were marked with the sign of the cross. Seeing a resemblance to the Crusaders' shields, Francis took the dream to mean he should fight in the Crusades.

Not only was he without his soldier's mantle, but also he then lost the one thing that would allow him to fight in the Crusades: his health. Yet, out of a desire for fame and the glory of battle, he set out with other young men from Assisi to join the Crusaders' armies. However, his sickness returned, ending his quest to fight in God's army, at least in the way he thought.

As he slept one night, a voice again spoke to him saying that he had misunderstood the first dream. He should return home. There he would form an army of his own, each of his followers wearing the sign of the cross, but not one carrying a sword or a shield.

Back to Assisi

Francis returned through Assisi's gate and was soon in his own home again, lying in his bed, being nursed to health by his mother, who made certain he rested and ate well. As he recovered, his heart moved toward God.

He grew stronger, and he began to find quiet places outside town where he prayed. One day, alone in one of these spots, he looked up and saw before him Jesus as he was nailed to the cross. As Francis saw God's all-out love for him, his soul melted. And whenever this image came to mind, he could not keep from tears. From that day on, he lived his life to reflect God's love.

San Damiano

Not long after this, Francis rode his horse into a pasture near Assisi. He came upon what he feared more than the enemy charging in battle: a leper. Gathering courage to overcome his natural fear of sickness and death, he dismounted, approached the leper, and kissed him.

This incident gave Francis a new and very different work. He gave up war and began to serve sick people in hospitals, and especially lepers in the lazar houses where they were made to stay. He gave them his clothing and what money he had. He washed and treated the lepers' wounds and hugged them, despite the danger of his becoming ill, because of his compassion and warmth.

One day, praying in the dilapidated San Damiano church, Francis heard a voice from the painted crucifix telling him, "Repair my church." These same words were spoken three times. He took this as a literal command and obeyed, hurrying to his home to gather some of his father's expensive fabrics. Then, riding to a nearby town, he sold his horse and the fabrics and used the money to buy materials he needed to begin repairing the church.

Pietro Bernardone, filled with rage, appealed to the bishop. Although the bishop was more understanding of Francis, he told him he must return the money to his father, since it was unjustly gained. Francis once again obeyed, giving his father not only the money, but also the clothes he was wearing, saying that they too belonged to his father.

Francis, given a worn servant's shirt by the kind bishop, walked out, looking for a place to stay while continuing his work. If God gave him a job to do, God would provide all he would need to do it.

Some robbers met him on the road and asked him, "Who are you?" Francis answered, "I am the herald of the Great King!" The bandits beat him and threw him into a ditch filled with snow. But Francis simply pulled himself out, brushed off the snow, and continued on his path, singing praise to God.

At a monastery on the way, Francis was given another worn servant's shirt and a meal in exchange for some work. With no resources of his own, Francis begged townspeople for stones or money to use for restoring the church. He set about the work and kept at it until all was repaired from top to bottom, front to back. This building is where Francis's friend Clare would soon begin the sister order that was inspired by Francis's *Rule* (a guide for religious living).

After finishing the work on San Damiano, he restored a broken-down chapel, Portiuncula (Our Lady of the Angels), which became the place from which his followers were sent out and then returned. After two years of rebuilding many churches, he made a small mud-and-straw hut near this small chapel to sleep in. And from this hut his larger work began.

Italy

On St. Matthias's feast day, Francis took the Gospel reading as a direction to imitate Jesus's life as closely as he could: free from all possessions, trusting God his Father for food and all his needs.

Francis gave away even his sandals, walking stick, and belt, and wore only a brown wool tunic tied with a cord.

Walking through fields and towns, Francis called the people to make a new start: to love Christ with all they were and with all they had. And many did, when they heard his words and watched his life. Francis respected and loved each person and greeted anyone he met saying, "Peace and all good."

Bernard of Quintavalle, one of Assisi's richest men, was curious about the former fun-loving, free-spending, finely dressed Francis giving up his wealth, caring for lepers—telling all to love Christ with their whole life.

So, Bernard invited Francis to spend the night in his home. When all were asleep but he and Francis, both pretended to be snoring to lead the other into thinking he was sound asleep. Bernard wanted secretly to hear Francis pray. As soon as Francis heard his host snore, he rose to pray, thinking he would pray in secret. The young saint was overcome with the goodness of God and repeatedly said out loud to him, "My God and my all!" The rich man was so moved by Francis's prayer of five words that he asked to join him in following Christ.

Bernard sold his possessions, gave all his money to Assisi's poor, became Francis's first companion, and remained his lifelong friend.

Within a year, the number of Francis's followers had grown to eleven. He called them "Little Brothers." All agreed to follow a Rule to remain free from possessions and marriage, trusting God for all their needs. They were free to go anywhere at any time to preach and serve without worry, often singing as they went.

Francis and the Friars Minor ("Little Brothers") soon made their way to Rome to seek the Pope's approval. At first the Pope was hesitant because Francis's life sounded too severe. But in a dream the Pope saw a man poorly dressed like a shepherd, whom he recognized as Francis, propping up one of the grand churches of Rome that was about to fall down. When he awoke, the Pope approved Francis's Rule, commissioning him and his followers to preach and call for people to repent.

The members of the young order, growing in numbers, walked throughout Italy preaching that Christ loved all, washing the diseased skin of lepers, and working in farmers' fields in exchange

for meals. If there was no work, the Little Brothers might beg, but only for a meal, never for money.

Townspeople and priests listened and wanted to love Christ in the same way. Some followed Francis and some supplied meals and shelter for Francis and his friends.

Francis loved the Little Brothers, sometimes by correcting them and sometimes by encouraging them. Once, a young follower was afraid that he wasn't meeting Francis's expectations and became discouraged. When Francis heard of this, he went to the young brother and assured him that he was among the dearest to him, and told him to come anytime to see him. Then he added, "From friendship, learn faith."

Another time, Francis taught a certain Little Brother using questions and life experience itself.

Francis and Brother Leo, who listened carefully to Francis and wrote down many things he said, were walking down a muddy road on a cold, rainy night. Brother Leo asked, "What is perfect joy?" Francis answered, "If, when we arrive at our destination, we knock at the gate and the porter angrily asks, 'Who are you?', and we tell him, 'We are two of the Little Brothers,' and he angrily answers, 'You are liars, acting like brothers to get food and a warm place to stay. Go away!', and if we accept this injustice with patience, without getting mad or talking back, believing the porter really knows we are who we say we are, and that it is God who makes him speak against us to test our faith, then write it down, Brother Leo: 'That is perfect joy.'"

And Beyond

After preaching throughout Italy, Francis sent groups of Little Brothers to Spain and Germany and others to Hungary and England, often singing on their way.

Eventually, they would be called Franciscans.

Francis knew God's love was for all people. He did not want to stop at the nearby countries. He even sent some of his brothers, who now numbered in the thousands, to the North African countries of Tunisia and Morocco. There, they told the people about Jesus, who died for them also, and about the love of God that brought Francis to tears.

Egypt

The Crusader armies were then at war with the Saracens in Damietta, Egypt, not far from the Holy Land.

Francis, with a small number of companions, traveled by ship to reach the Sultan Malek al-Kamil, to tell him of God's love so that he and his people could be saved and the war might be ended.

Francis and his friends arrived at the Crusaders' camp, and with two of the brothers, he started out to the sultan's headquarters. The Crusaders were unhappy to see Francis. They wanted only to fight. The Saracens were confused to see Francis, but they presented him to the sultan.

Francis explained the Christian faith to Malek al-Kamil, even offering to walk into fire to prove its truth. The sultan greatly admired Francis's courage, and his heart was warmed by Francis's desire that he be saved.

The sultan's admiration of Francis resulted in allowing him to continue his travel to the Holy Land.

To this day, Franciscans are the custodians of the sacred places in the Holy Land—including in Jerusalem, Nazareth, and Bethlehem—where Jesus lived, taught, and healed. They are men of peace.

Return to Italy

Francis took the next two years to travel the length of Italy. He started from the south as far as Catania and continued north as far as Bologna, proclaiming the great love and goodness of God. He urged people to start afresh, giving God their lives in return for such love.

During this time, he also wrote a more formal Rule for his growing religious order, which had spread to many other countries. This revised Rule followed the first, requiring brothers to own nothing except their rough Franciscan robes and to remain unmarried. The new Rule was approved by the Pope.

A Second Order was started for women who wanted to make the same vow: to own nothing and to remain unmarried. Francis's friend Clare was the first member of this order.

Then, Francis created a Third Order for those who lived normal lives with families and houses and work, but were inspired by the life and preaching of Francis to give themselves to God completely.

Greccio

One year, near the time of Christmas, Francis and his companions came to Greccio, a town built into the side of a cliff, where they had a rough shelter reserved for whenever they came through. Francis was determined to create a living scene of Jesus's birth in Bethlehem to help the people of Greccio understand how God humbled himself in sending his Son to be born as a baby and lie in a feeding trough between an ox and a donkey.

Finding a suitable cave-like stable and manger, the Little Brothers acted the parts of shepherds and Joseph. A young mother of Greccio was chosen to take the part of Mary, and her baby, the part of Jesus. Francis led the midnight service. A live ox and a donkey on either side of the manger simply acted as themselves.

This was the very first Nativity crèche.

Home to Portiuncula

Francis was forty-four years old, and was very tired from his years of traveling to tell others of God's love, remembering all his life his first vision of Jesus on the cross. He traveled in rain, snow and ice, burning heat, and often without food. He had pushed to the limit his very weary body, which he referred to as a donkey—an animal that spent its life carrying heavy loads or pulling a plow for its master without receiving any thanks.

Francis and Brother Leo had gone north from Assisi to pray and fast. It was while they were on Mount La Verna that a six-winged angel, called a seraph, appeared to Francis, and gave him the gift of the five wounds Christ suffered on the cross.

 24

Thereafter, Francis always covered the wounds on his hands, feet, and side, to keep them a secret, but he counted them as gifts allowing him to share in Jesus's suffering.

Besides his worn-out body, Francis was now going blind from a painful eye disease that no treatments of his time could cure. For a while, he was taken to San Damiano to be cared for by Clare and her Sisters of the Second Order. During this time, he wrote his famous "Canticle of the Creatures."

At last, his friends brought their beloved Francis back to Portiuncula, laying him on his crude bed in the hut next to the church he had restored some twenty years earlier when he first began imitating Jesus's life—free from all possessions.

God had provided for his needs as well as those of his Little Brothers, the Sisters, and all who had chosen to follow this way of life. They were always calling for people to make a new start: to love Christ with all they were and all they had. Many did, and many still do.

When Francis recognized his body was nearing the end, he asked to be placed on the ground wearing only his long, rough robe. Then, with his closest companions around him singing the "Canticle of the Creatures," he asked that Psalm 142 be read as well.

"Lead my soul out of prison so that
I may give praise to Your name."

And with the words of that psalm, Francis went home to God, whose love he had lived to repay by imitating Jesus's life as closely as he could and trusting God his Father who had provided for all his needs.

THE END